LAW & SIDE-LAW

LAW & SIDE-LAW

Family Hostility / Family Empathy

by aaron w wemple

Clean Law Family / Social Enterprise – St. Louis

Law & Side-Law

Family Hostility / Family Empathy

Published by Clean Law in 2020

ISBN: 978-0-578-76468-9

1. Family & Relationships 2. Social Science   3. Science
4. Technology & Engineering   5. Education

Printed in the United States of America

For more information:

Clean Law Family / Social Enterprise

www.cleanlaw.today

Dedicated to permanently
"up-law" children of deployed,
divorced, lost or separated parents.

Contents

The Worst Separation Pains Ever?

Law v. Law – State $

Side-Law – 360° Solutions / Savings

New Skills, New Deals, New Economy

Preface

Since beginning of time through the rise of military deployment wars, divorce court battles, school strikes, and social unrest, the psychological safety nets associated with children involved with these high-conflict severances have gotten thinner and thinner. Many of us as children have experienced the permanent impacts and post trauma from dangerous and difficult divisive contracts deals, policies and their resulting treaties. Fights and overlapping hostilities until one side or the other can no longer fight anymore and eventually gives up.

But today these disconnecting protocols are receiving increased attention by researchers. Proof of this mandate for our children suggests that some kids do suffer more from these situations than others (Tashiro et al., 2006). While new safety shelters to better protect the middle grey areas of debates are very much in queue, but still excluded in everyday policy-making. This book introduces the Superdivergence Warning Scale, child safety files (starting and ending with overlapping empathy) relief.

Since I survived the conventional "family" law v. law valleys, I give special thanks to people in those systems today who are left out and give people like me reasons to pivot the status quote. I personally would like to thank Montgomery County, Illinois retired courtroom officials, Christian County, Illinois retired courtroom authors, Macon County, Illinois leaders, SIU-E, Millikin University, and many others who casually fired me from life and a healthy career simply for following the law, but who also inspired me to try and help prevent these invisible things that happen in the trunks of systems from happening to other people. Those experiences tend to either kill a person or thicken their intellectual skin.

I'd especially like to thank team CLU (Clean Law Union) reuniting ministry and Water Street Mission homeless shelter in Decatur, IL who helped me understand that it takes a team to survive down-law systems – getting pushed harder and harder while you're already down in a valley. The compacting trunk of justice with no authentic way out until now.

And thanks to ITEN and all of the other business venture support organizations in or near the Cortex district of St. Louis, Mo for helping startup businesses like Clean Law Family / Social Enterprise develop.

Aaron W. Wemple

Introduction

You didn't get into a relationship or organization just to fight situational differences, intimidation factors, lawyers, and judges. Likewise, the Re-Re-Re-Re-Redacted Life chapter of this book is but a brief part of my (Aaron Wemple) experience, and many other people's experiences, with our various branches of schools and governments. Especially conventional "family" law v. law and policy. Civilians like us routinely, sometimes automatically stained beyond stained in terms of our perceived "American Dream" (and then lack thereof), our perceived "parental" sustainability (and then lack thereof), and in terms of our perceived "civility" (and then lack thereof). It's the reason why so many of us have been forced to become "champions for children" and lay down our lives instead so that every child can have a family. Even if it means phenomenal new organic childhood, family and community developments.

When you're a child and you dream of becoming an astronaut, you may never find out the right steps along the way of life to get you there. And billions of different people are most likely going to mislead you away from your dream in a billion different ways. That's parenting in our world.

And if you're a child whose family is living on the edge of sustainability by being tried with a military deployment war or high-conflict divorce battle, and you dream of a day to stay connected to both of your first loves in your life – both of your parents, then a billion different people, millions policies and an infinite number of positions and excuses are going to mislead you a zillion different ways. None of them with authentic "connection-keeping" gravity. All of them hostile towards your family, and your own family ability. But why? That's what we've now uncovered.

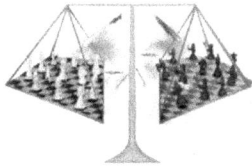

It was the summer of 1992. It was not only hot outside; it was heated inside of my family too. That year our lives were turned forever inside-out.

And then eventually it was the summer of 2010 when my dreams died. Old societies and conventional systems are in no way compatible with organic childhood safety of loving their own hopes and dreams.

So, many of us were forced to ask ourselves, why do we feel so much different than everyone else? Why does searching for help come back on us and make us feel so much more different and distressed inside? Why does not having a big, powerful position, a black robe, a badge, uniform, pedestal, prestige, paycheck, microphone, and mountains of clerks / supporting ulterior systems make us empathy filers feel so bad? Because empathy outside of family does not exist.

Maybe the American dream is dead upon arrival in some arenas. Maybe it is time to re-imagine childhood protection, childproof policies, and the American Dream?

Why couldn't our initial divorce filing, like other protocols, include empathy, inclusion, open and level discussions like sitting at the dining room table? Because there's no money or power in that. And, there's an endless supply of money keeping young families in the trench, especially people in desperate situations who desperately need answers.

Does your family have a free private child safety file shelter yet?

Today, someone is really thinking of you and yours. Not $ to permanently separate the two. It's your serendipity, and you need it now! Law & Side-Law brings life into families, and broken families back to life in a simple way. By opening up the treasure chest of organic facts that we tightly lock away in the financial, social and emotional trunks of justice.

14

The Worst Separation Pains Ever?

(Source: cleanlaunion.today, 2020)

Shadow & Light

1. Stubs and the Stubbed

"Bats and the batted"

180-degree "law v. law" they pen, "It's the safest form of clarity!"
    But stubs and the stubbed make us hurt like bats and the batted.
The ole "haves and have-nots," they cry, "It's just the way it is!"
    Yet, 360-degrees, obviously, is safer for the kids.

    Like eating someone else's left-over pizza;
        And a fresh meal for you;
    Like drinking someone else's backwash
        And a side of clean drinking water too.

    Law & Side-Law;
        Our country, our country;
    'Tis of thee, 'tis of thee;
        Files of fighting, files of liberty.

    Like living in someone else's house;
        And a side house for you;
    Like wearing someone else's clothes;
        And side clothes for you.

    Like sleeping someone else's sleep;
        And side sleep of your own;
    Like making someone else's love;
        And making love for you.

    Like raising someone else's kid;
        And a side of raising your own kids too;
    Like getting "thought" on 💩;
        And side thoughts too 💡.

Like trusting someone else's security;
    And side security of your own;
Like working someone else's job;
    And a side business for you.

Like knowing someone else's money;
    And side money for you;
Like counting on someone else's insurance;
    And side insurance for you too.

Like enjoying someone else's property;
    And side property for you;
Like being a friend of a friend;
    And having some friends too.

Like seeing other people gain respect;
    And earning respect too;
Like seeing a job well-done;
    And getting a job done too.

Like seeing another people honored;
    And you feeling honor too;
Like experiencing another people's strength;
    And having strength too.

Like watching someone else's freedom;
    And a side of freedom for you;
Like seeing some else promoted;
    And a side promotion too.

180-degrees they publish, "It's the safest form of civility!"
    And now with side-law, there's a new publishing tree;
The ole "haves and have-nots," they cried, "It's just the way it is."
    And 360-degrees, obviously, is safer for you and me.

After side-law is the new deal, then we'll all sing songs of joyful empathy. Because without it, we're all feeling the gloom and doom of hostility. An old place where conducting yourself is like trying to catch up to a Tesla car while stuck in a horse and buggy always fighting about who's going to be the horse and who's going to be the buggy. Ouch and ouch in that race to some undefined finish line.

So, laugh your way from distress to clarity. Past the un-kept fields of nothingness. Saving the princess of data, while shooting past the firing lines, mountains and valleys of 180° divisions. Enjoying the sweat pursuit of happiness with effective 360° safer solutions for all. Law & Side-Law offers hope and healing at the intersection of law v. law - where healthy nuclear family roots used to be.

Not state or bar associated legal instruments and judicial mechanics, but organic and natural side-lawyering. Not injury lawyers but achievement lawyers. Not insults to injuries but value to preventions. Not vertical 180-degree differences between powerful positions and powerless parents, but open access. Not 180-degree horizontal party pipeline differences, but humanity. And not situational 180-degree barriers, but safer 360-degree perspectives. By those of us who were previously dead to the "family" law v. law systems. Dead without cause. Law & Side-Law introduces hope and healing at the intersection of law v. law - where healthy nuclear family roots used to be.

Law & Side-Law is innovative side-lawyering from an organic network with only organic points of views. Like washing your hands and wearing a mask to prevent the spread of Covid-19.

"Great and marvelous are your deeds, Lord God Almighty. Just and true are your ways, King of the nations. Who will not fear you, Lord, and bring glory to your name? For you alone are holy. All nations will come and worship before you, for your righteous acts have been revealed." (Rev. 15:3-4).

(Illustration courtesy: Varunjyoti Deori / www.blinkmotion.com)

Law & Side-Law - Going from family hostility (think horse and buggy) to familiy empathy (think advanced luxury car) to your finish line.

2. School Problems

Since the rise of military deployment wars and divorce battles, the psychological safety contract terms associated with children involved with high-conflict parental dissolutions are receiving increased attention by researchers. Proof from this literature suggests that some children suffer more from the difficulties of parental separations, deployment and divorce than others (Tashiro et al., 2006). Like poisonous wasps flying around outside of their homes, children need shelter from these mandated high-conflict situations outside of their direct environments.

Every year, one out of ten children grades K-12 will experience classical family separation and divorce, according to St. Angelo (2019). About 15-30% of those, she says, will be subjected to high conflict dynamics like anger, mistrust, and elevated stress.

Over a million children and their families have now experienced the stress and strains from the military deployment with their family members during the recent Iraq and Afghanistan war alone (McFarlane, 2009).

Studies also show that adolescents and emerging adults involved with divorce showed a significant increase in violent thoughts and a substantial decrease in academic preparedness (Neighbors et al. 1992). And while children themselves don't choose divorce, there are very limited self-reporting tools for children in the middle of those dynamics to allow parents, caseworkers, and psychology professionals to authentically identify children who may be at risk for long-term negative mental health consequences.

This paper will examine the design of self-reporting technology, such as the existing parental self-reporting smartphone application (the Custody Transfer Log, developed in partnership with the Chair of Mass Communications, Dr. Musonda Kapatamoyo, SIUE) and studies regarding the psychological impacts of high-conflict divorce situations on children.

3. Social Background

Researchers have found several conditions that may affect how well children can be expected to cope with divorce. Since 1970 the rates of divorce have been on the rise. The divorce rate was 4 in 1,000 marriages during the 1970s, according to Rogers (2010). By the year 2010, that rate had nearly tripled to 11.1 per 1,000 marriages. Furthermore, there are no "Rules of the Dissolution Road" book or course taught in school to help adolescents and emerging adults understand what to expect and how to function accordingly. This means that a life wreck is of less importance to our public safety concerns than an automobile wreck.

Sadly, collaborators should note that the market says divorce is a financial industry. And that the market is silent about parallel financial gravity to hold families together in unity. The amount of pay in the divorce industry is tied to slowly wrenching parents apart over time; it's never related to mending or holding families together quickly. And unlike criminal law, it is self-evident in classical family law cases that children and their conflicted, or cooperating parents are without several conflict reducing components like the right to be represented when they are poor. There is also no right to bail when parents accuse each other. There is no right to a jury supported decision regardless. There is no right to redress for any financial terms that are in concrete contracts which also have no termination dates. There's no investigations and many other heartbreaking conflict enhancers in context of childhood that we as a society don't even let guilty criminals like Ted Bundy walk through alone (Abel & Rettig, 2006). (Even though children of these families have themselves, homes, family careers, educations, and family retirement accounts all on the chopping block). Vital components which may escalate conflicts like agents gearing up two boxers for a prizefight. Lebow and Slesinger (2016) call divorce, its filings, and its activities "unretractable". A risk to children is the increased lethality associated with parents tearing each other apart with mechanical help according to Creig (2012).

In contrast to divisive principles, other researchers have found correlates of what they call stress-related growth in children of divorce (Tashiro et al., 2006). Challenging social and legal maneuvers by parents of divorce to their children may feel like being inside of two crashing automobiles at once. If children, who are the most fragile, gain even calloused insights, then that growth needs to be shared for the public good.

Thus, a different population that may have been previously underground and shushed while only knowing the revolving clashes of conflicts may also be on the cusp of shining new light on these experiences in a most helpful way. Self-reporting, therefore, may provide the only factual data that can help researchers and policymakers better understand the full effects divorce has on children. Terrell (2015) teaches research students that "the problem is the problem." He says that academic research is composed of its background, the problem itself, and the significance of the problem.

There are other factors that may lower the incidence of dysfunction in children of divorce and parental separations. In much of the early research, there were no distinctions made among the levels of conflicts (Johnson 1994). It should be noted that the ages of children when they become involved in a divorce or separation may affect how they respond to the experience. Different individuals react to the same stimuli in different manners. Which makes it hard, if not impossible to share consciousness. Likewise, different individuals may have different levels of tolerance to conflicts. The initial conflicts of divorce commonly wain two and half years after the initial filing and settle into what experts call parallel parenting (Johnson 1994). New trends also research the severity of conflicts during different age groups of children (Pruett & Barker, 2009). Furthermore, longitudinal studies since the prevalence of divorce are just now coming available.

Finally, besides the problem of no real-time measurement tools, it seems just as futile but at the same time vital to reimagine nuclear family "disengagements." Disengagements, in the first half of this paper, refers to a parent and a child living a considerable distance apart (Hetherington & Kelly, 2003). In the second half of this paper, both disengagements and connection-keeping refer to problems and designing missing components between children and their parents. For example, before a new real-time mobile app was launched there was no custody transfer evidence, but now a digitized custody transfer log exists. Furthermore, disengaged phone lines between children and their parents could theoretically harness a connection-keeping component rendering and open telecommunication network. Financial impasses could be re-designing into functional financial veins. Mail delivery obstructions could pivot into normal mail delivery. Tricked away visitations could be kept with virtual holographic visitations. Closed problem fears could span with open minded solution-thinking. Seemingly ordinary disengagement-to-engagement continuums between a child and both parents to reconsider, especially when designing updates to practices, programs, and policies for the next-generation of children of high-conflict (HC) dissolutions. The number and magnitude of these disengagements would be particularly useful tools, especially since the disengagement components are more prevalent in HC dissolutions than in amicable, cooperative co-parenting (CC).

4. Landmark Research

Research on the effects of HC divorces involving children is in its infancy. In 1996 the first landmark 25-year longitudinal study of 131 children called the "California Children of Divorce Study" finished. In the research, Pioneering Psychologist Judith Wallerstein investigated the effects divorce has on children (Karen & Flowers, 2018). A project that many following researchers say broke through the stigma of divorce and its mislabeled children meaning new grounds to build on.

Wallerstein found that the impacts on children from divorce are cumulative (Karen & Flowers, 2018). At first, children are shaken and feel socially out of place when the separation occurs. But the vibrations of that experience crescendo over time into adulthood. Wallerstein discovered by following the group that through each of life's stages, from childhood, adolescence, emerging adulthood, and adulthood, the divorce is experienced in new and different ways. In each step comprising their emotional stability, ability to trust, and expectations (Karen & Flowers, 2018)

The research means that throughout various stages in life, especially in adulthood, issues like anger may be prevalent. Many participants in the study group eventually said that they have no intention of helping their parents when they are old (Karen & Flowers, 2018). However, current research on children of divorce still focuses on the adverse effects of divorce, and not the positive results or the growth that some children experience (Tashiro et al. 2006).

5. Research Engagement

This brief period in time where research finally exists on the effects of the intensities of divorce on children tends to focus on the negativities and gives little attention to the positive developments at the end of an unhappy marriage (Hetherington & Kelly, 2003). Contemporary research suggests that the direst and the most optimistic generalizations regarding the impact of divorce on children should be challenged. Group averages speak to broadly paint individual men, women, girls, and boys in terms of unhealthy dysfunctions while also concealing good and unique coping skills. Interviews during a nearly thirty-year study at the University of Virginia suggests that cooperative parental relationships are often the missing ingredient for healthy children of divorce (Hetherington & Kelly, 2003).

Beginning in 1973 with 144 couples (along with a comparison group of intact nuclear families) who were experiencing a divorce took part in a longitudinal study at the University of Virginia (Hetherington & Kelly, 2003). As the research progressed, the scope was expanded in additional projects including some 1,400 families. Later research incorporated adult children from the original families, and stepfamilies who were unrelated to the first group.

Hetherington and Kelly (2003) define a "generous attitude" as ex-spouses who have the ability to manage their communication and cooperation. Research shows that 25% of divorced families maintain a generous attitude towards each other in which they talk over the children's issues, coordinate household rules, co-develop child-rearing practices, and adjust to fit their children's needs. This means that 25% of divorced families remain engage in various and meaningful ways after a divorce.

By the time children of divorce reach the age of 15, divorced fathers live an average of 400 miles away studies show (Hetherington & Kelly, 2003). Hetherington and Kelly (2003) define "disengagement" as the point (on average 75 miles) in which parents are less inclined to visit. The emotional consequences of disengagement reflect in the interviews with adult children who are disengaged (Hetherington & Kelly, 2003). The study shows that parents who remain in the same area after a divorce improves the chances of their children coping well. 1 in 4 females from divorced families and 1 in 3 males feel very close to their fathers. Whereas 7 out of 10 adult children from intact nuclear families feel very close to

29

their fathers (Hetherington & Kelly, 2003), which means that the study has the potential for social policy initiatives for either raising awareness or else regulating disengagement limits for childhood safety.

6. Profiling Severities

A more recent study aimed to identify post-divorce co-parenting profiles and differentiate between children's psychological adjustments to each (Lamela et al., 2015). Researchers had been guided by previous findings that co-parenting is the crucial mechanism for predicting the outcomes of children of divorce (Feinberg, 2003).

The study presents a cluster analysis from 314 divorced parents. They tested for evidence of distinct co-parenting profiles and whether these profiles relate to children's internalizing and externalizing problems (Lamela et al., 2015).

Overall, the results yielded and later replicated three distinct post-divorce co-parenting profiles: a high-conflict co-parenting group, an undermining co-parenting group, and a cooperative co-parenting group. Each group was then compared to levels of children internalizing and externalizing their problems.

Cooperating co-parents where finally associated with low levels of children internalizing their problems, compared to HC and undermining co-parenting. Children of cooperating co-parents also exhibited low levels of externalizing problems compared to undermining co-parents. This study shows that cooperating co-parenting profile is significantly associated with lower levels of children's adjustment problems.

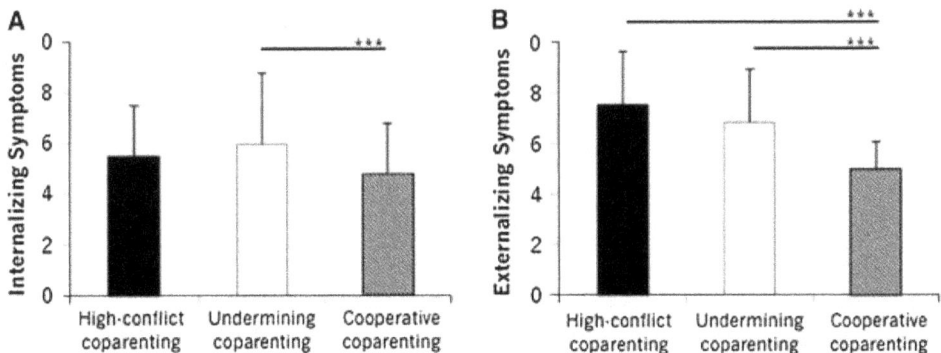

(Source: https://link.springer.com/article/10.1007/s10578-015-0604-5, 2016)

Law v. Law – State $

7. Behavioral and Academic Differences

In a Swiss study, researchers wanted to examine the differences between children of divorced parents and children of intact nuclear families to see if there were any differences in anxiety, self-esteem, and degree of behavioral problems (Schick, 2002). An area of research that may be important to reduce social violence and increase academic preparedness by spotlighting any differences between children of divorce and children of intact families. Previous studies also investigated statically significant differences, whereas this study examined any differences concerning clinical significance.

Another reason for the Swiss study was that many previous findings indicated that children of divorce have a predisposition for behavioral problems. Because in addition to normal developmental processes, children of divorce have to cope with additional developmental demands like juggling multiple homes. The results of previous longitudinal studies and reviews suggests that the stress experienced after separation results in negative outcomes in behavior, self-esteem, social relations, mental health, and academic status (Schick, 2002).

The Swiss study surveyed 241 children ages nine to 13 years old. One hundred seventy-five were from intact nuclear families and 66 from divorce. They recruited participants through newspaper advertisements, flyers, and letters addressed personally to parents and handed out through teachers at school. The children who participated were asked questions in class or small groups and given rewards of extra credit or a little present for participating in the survey.

The Swiss study yielded two clinically significant differences from the self-reporting perspectives of two groups of children. One difference was that children of divorced homes face more significant social anxiety than their peers from intact families. And the second difference was that children of divorce homes experience reduced academic performance. These two findings of 14 proposed adverse effects also indicative of statistically significant differences between children of divorce and children of intact nuclear families (Schick, 2002).

The behavioral and academic differences between children of divorce and children of intact families mean that differences are not the result of separation or divorce per se, but a consequence of limited social support and the children's perception of interparental conflict (Schick,

2002). And although the dysfunctions can begin from divorce, research shows that in addition to quantitative methods, qualitative methods should be applied (Schick, 2002).

8. Stress-Related Growth

Because research in this area is relatively new, and most studies are geared towards the adverse effects of divorce, few studies have specifically asked about the positive impact on children from divorce. Fewer yet propose a means to measure those positive effects. However, research does suggest that posttraumatic growth happens in the form of personal growth (Tashiro, et al., 2006). Albeit, sometimes it's a resentful and socially abnormal growth.

Researchers conducted a meta-analysis looking for commonly reported changes from children in their relationships with their parents following a divorce. Two meta-analytic studies compared children of divorced and intact families in terms of parent-child relationships. In other surveys, researchers asked parents about positive aspects of their relationships with their children following a divorce (Tashiro, et al., 2006).

Studies found that compared to children of intact nuclear families, children of divorced homes report somewhat better relationships with their mothers and fathers after a divorce. For example, in one study, children from divorced homes reported a better parent-child relationship than did children from unhappy intact homes (Tashiro, et al., 2006). Children of divorce have also reported growth in relationship skills, which includes being more compassionate, empathetic, and understanding. Similar growths had been reported in their relationships with their siblings, which included love, loyalty, and more tolerance.

When parents are asked what qualities, their children acquire as a result of adjusting to divorce, the most common reaction (73%) is that their children become more independent and mature. Wallerstein noticed that "many" of the children in her study described themselves as having adjusted stronger and more independent as a result of their increased responsibilities. Wallerstein and other researchers also note that sometime down the road, children may resent growing up too fast and missing out on childhood (Tashiro, et al., 2006).

The most significant gap in research appears to be what children experience at the time of divorce compared to their peers and what they report later on in life about that experience - of course, reporting on facts after the fact is notoriously biased. There are no universal assessment standards to measure and store the growth of children from the situation

(Tashiro, et al., 2006) in real-time. No studies were found regarding positive academic growth, which could mean opportunity.

9. Significance of the Problem

The overriding legal standard that governs the high-conflict divorce decisions is the best interests of the child. However, neither states nor local courts define best interest, but instead provide a list of factors from the state statutes to be considered in each case (Austin, Fieldstone, et al., 2013). Research shows that a common best interest factor in some states is the extent to which each parent can support and encourage the other parent's relationship with their child (Austin, Fieldstone, et al., 2013). This is known as the "friendly parent doctrine." In many states like Florida, for example, a specific factor in state statute F.S. § 61.13(2)(c)(1) reads: "It is the public policy of this state that each minor child has frequent and continuing contact with both parents after the parents separate or the marriage of the parties is dissolved and to encourage parents to share the rights and responsibilities, and joys, of childrearing. There is no presumption for or against the father or mother of the child or for or against any specific time-sharing schedule when creating or modifying the parenting plan of the child" (Austin, Fieldstone, et al., 2013). This statutory factor in more state statute's and therefore more courts, would mean parent neutrality, that each parent could justifiably support the other parent-child relationship, social benevolence, less conflict, decreased childhood violence, and increased academic preparedness.

Children's acclimation to divorce isn't only influenced by individual characteristics and context, but also by the relations between the family members and their propensity towards conflict and cooperation (Kalter et al., 1989). Researchers believe that interparental strife is the leading cause of the adverse effects of divorce on children (Kalter et al., 1989; Schick, 2002). Above all, it is the way that conflicts are incurred that's important for children's mental health and development (Kalter et al., 1989). Gauging, reducing, or reducing the propensity for interparental conflict in some way, shape, or form may be paramount to reducing the violent thoughts and increasing the academic preparedness of children.

10. The Gatekeeping Process

Researchers define parental gatekeeping as the attitudes and actions that serve to affect the quality of the other parent's relationships with the child (Austin, Pruett, et al., 2013). Gatekeeping is a research-based concept which initially examined intact nuclear families from the perspective of a mothers' influence over father-child relationships and, conversely, from the perspective of a father's influence over mother-child relationships (Austin, Pruett, et al., 2013). A theory gate-opening and gate-closing in those relationships where one party or the other sees their role as the primary caregiver and therefore "manager" of the child or specific situations. Such influence is arguably present in any relationship.

The reason that the study of gatekeeping is important to childhood adjustment is because when the influence of one parent on the other detracts from the other's relationship with the child, then it's the child who witnesses the attitude and any physical disengagements. Thus, slowing or inhibiting necessary adjustments (Austin, Pruett, et al., 2013). It's also important because gatekeeping can be intertwined with HC co-parenting (Austin, Pruett, et al., 2013).

11. The Gatekeeping Products

Researchers collaborated with practitioners to outline a typology of gatekeeping to help better understand and resolve custody disputes (Austin, Pruett, et al., 2013). Facilitative gatekeeping is that which is described in state's list of best interest factors. As noted previously, in Florida statute the first best interest factor is both parent's abilities to support each other's child rearing role. That's state statute facilitated gatekeeping. Restrictive gatekeeping, on the other hand, refers to activities by a parent that intends to interfere or does interfere with the other parent's engagements with the child. Restrictive gatekeeping predictably negatively influences that relationship between the parent and child and the child (Austin, Pruett, et al., 2013). Research has shown that restrictive gatekeeping is more common with HC parenting, and that bilateral restrictive gatekeeping can occur when enduring HC situations occur (Austin, Pruett, et al., 2013).

Studies have proven that most parents are cooperative cooperants (CC) (Austin et al., 2013). Sometimes they increasingly disengaged from each other and communicate on a very limited basis. Judges and case workers, therefore, can administer assessments and evaluations to try and shine a light on gate-opening, gate-closing, and theoretical pinch pints (Austin, Pruett, et al., 2013). Judges can also ask that the reports delineate specific gate-opening and gate-closing behaviors of each parent and behavioral or academic status of children (Austin, Pruett, et al., 2013). This means that the gatekeeping model is a uniform way for judges and other decision-makers to think about the best interest standard in those states.

12. Gatekeeping Environments

In fears of a HC environment or a legal issue in court, an analysis of the gatekeeping scenario helps address questions about how facilitative (assuming that's a factor) or restrictive a parent is toward the role of the other co-parent (Austin et al., 2013). This research was conducted because it was said that courts will want to know if restrictive gatekeeping behaviors are tied to the immediately opened divorce case or if they are likely to endure.

Researchers developed a continuum for parallel consultation practice (Austin et al., 2013). A range in attitudes and or actions from facilitative gatekeeping (FG) to restrictive gatekeeping (RG). They found five ranges from very facilitative, cooperative, disengaged, restrictive, and very restrictive. For example, one parent may be very facilitative, or inclusive, of the other parent. While another parent may be very restrictive, or derogates, the other parent. While still another parent may be perfectly in the middle range and laissez faire.

Use and research of this continuum is still in the early stage. But studies show best long-term adjustment occurs when children have quality relationship with both parents, and when parents exhibit cooperational coparenting (CC). While restrictive gatekeeping (RG) and bilateral RG is believed to foster HC, resulting in poor adjustment of children, unless they are shielded from the conflict by at least one parent (Austin et al., 2013).

Research shows that healthy developments in children are compromised whenever one or both parenting styles are harsh without sensitivity (Austin et al., 2013). Evidence also suggests that children who are exposed to conflict adjust poorly, unless they are shielded from the conflict by a parent's benevolent ability to keep the child from being the focus of, or involved in, the conflict (Austin et al., 2013).

The gatekeeping model, typology, continuum, and environment not only adds to the significance of the problem but broadens the view for decision makers to see the entire field of HC divorce with more dimensions. Its significance lends knowledge transferability to the integrative studies where psychology meets engineering. However, it also means that without a "friendly parent doctrine" best interest factor explicitly written in state statutes, then the gatekeeping factor is presumed to stand and be open and a child safety concern.

RGs during HCs may be important because it means that when these cases last long enough that a judge has to step in and render a decision based on the state's best interest factors, then the theoretical damage from disengagements to the child's relationships and behaviors have already been done.

The study of restrictive gatekeeping and later introduction of its social fabric mate called connection-keeping is also believed to help aid in the transfer of knowledge in this collaboration.

13. The Re-Re-Re-Re-Redacted Life

You didn't get into a relationship or organization just to fight situational differences, intimidation factors, lawyers, and judges. The re-re-re-re-redacted life lived can be the worst separation pains ever.

Likewise, this chapter is but a brief part of my (Aaron Wemple's) experiences, and of many others, with our judicial branch of government. Civilians feel it in terms of our perceived American Dream (and lack thereof), our family sustainability and then lack thereof), and in terms of our civility (and then lack thereof). It's the reason why many of us have become "champions for children" instead and want every child to have a family.

When you're a child and you dream of being an airplane pilot, you may never have the right steps presented to you to get there as you grow up. And billions of different people may mislead you in a billion different ways.

If you're a child whose family is living with a military deployment war or high-conflict divorce battle, and you dream of staying connected to your siblings, then billions of different people are going to mislead you a billion different ways. None of them authentic.

It was the summer of 1992. It was not only hot outside; it was heated inside of my house too. That year our lives were turned forever inside-out. My wife, at the time, and I were having marital problems. So I traveled as a concerned parent to our local "family" courthouse to try and help my family find a healthy answer for one difficult issue. A common belief in those days was that separating a family was better than my young wife and I fighting all the time and conflicting our son. Fighting, in our case, which led to Corey being lifted up off of the ground and pulled by one arm out the threshold of his home harshly. This escalation in fighting worried me not only for the safety of our child but the sustainability of our family and marriage. As an idealistic adolescent myself, I was pleased to begin working with the family law and family court systems. Both seemed to have the objective of helping us properly raise our young 2-year-old boy in his best interest. After a recent Illinois legislative battle, the organization known as Healthcare and Family Services (HFS) was a highly respected department in the state. Little did I know that separating was at the heart of what the "family" court did. Many counties in Illinois welcomed HFS assistance since it was known that they contracted child support with their institutional charts and federal funding. "Family Services" in my county implied that they could show young couples like us how to address one simple issue and become whole again.

Disillusionment came as we realized that the court system did not know how to help families like mine resolve their issues and those widespread sufferings. The problem of young people finding help for their family issues are much more complex and obstructive than many of us can imagine. Also, one of the principal dynamics of our county board and state general assembly are two political party protocols - to escalate divisiveness as a means of maintaining attention and policy-making power - often dominated our news and community concerns. There seemed to be no low-cost or inclusive space for simple help and simple answers to sometimes life-threatening marital problems.

More and more disillusionment's quickly wove themselves together over time like a strengthening vine when I looked at other struggling families, many of whom were my friends, some of whom took their own lives, and we realized together that "family law" and "family" court had many inherent problems of their own that had yet to be resolved. For example, why do guilty criminals have the right and the cash flow pipeline of a procedural safety net in the form of a counselor when they are poor but truly innocent parents, many of whom have children on the line, do not have that same safety net and that same cash flow pipeline for a safety net while in they are both in the same system, with the same procedures?

The "family law" practice and "family" court themselves faced many monumental problems of their own that had accompanied what some felt were cottages industries to protect those oversights- governmental sprawl and squalor, monumental disconnects, bias and discrimination, party-centric pipelines above all. So, I was forced to ask myself, what is family? Is it good or is it bad? Disillusionment's later evolved into disenfranchisement when I filed a legal "Civil Complaint" in the United States District Court for the Central District of Illinois (case number 3:2011cv03376) to get to the bottom of that issue. And to hopefully someday find an answer to the original question that I had asked back in 1994. It was now 2011 and eight months after that original "family" case was over in court (case number 06-f-66). Besides family, my second concern was for the sake of civility. It was unfortunately denied and relabeled by the judge as something that it wasn't. There's an old joke about the slowness of a snail. It goes like this. A lady was sitting at home when she hears a knock at the door. She opens the door and sees a small snail on the porch. She picks up the snail and throws it as far as she can. Two years later, there's another knock at the door. She opens it and sees the same snail again. And the snail says, "What was that all about?" The point being, it took the small snail two whole years to get back to the place where he could ask a civilized question again. Eight years after my first simple question, it evolved into having to knock and ask another door to let me in to try and answer what was now two questions. Can "Family law" help my issue, and can this court help me understand why a small civilized question was picked up and thrown as hard as it could be? Mistrust came again when I went to a second courthouse door that was even farther but seemed to be a possible answer to the first question and now to the second question. Although my child was grown up now and help with the first question was no longer relevant, I filed a second so called "Civil Complaint" in United States District Court case number 3:2013cv03015 to try and solve my second and now third questions - why my family and I weren't worthy of an answer, why civil court could not be civil, and why am I constantly being thrown out of contention? This time I added what I felt like was proof of my snailness compared to real people: Truly guilty criminals like mass murders have free legal; help to access and navigate the legal system for answers to questions and cases, but poor and truly innocent young parents do not have that same right in the same system. Needless to say, as a caring parent and a concerned citizen asking too many questions, I started getting locked up and hidden away. They made even my slimy appear toxic. I was thrown out of my life and lost everything and everyone. So, I was forced to ask myself, what is civility? Is it good or is it bad? I then moved near a third courthouse door and knocked again. I was thrown farther away yet. Then a fourth door, a fifth, and a sixth door. Every time I was thrown as far away as they could. The ole small snail had its trail of voided issues. And that's just one parent's worst nightmare. Just one parent's worst separation pains ever.

It was the summer of 2010 when my dreams died. Old societies and systems are obviously not be compatible with organic children loving their own dreams, families, and search for answers.

So, we're been forced to ask ourselves. Why do we feel so much differently than everyone else? Why does searching for help come back on us and make us feel so much more different inside? Why does not having a big, powerful position, a rope, badge, uniform, pedestal, prestige, paycheck, and mountains of clerks make us goo-goo-ers feel different?

Maybe the American dream is dead upon arrival in some areas. Maybe it is time we re-imagine childhood protection, family sustainability, and the American Dream?

Does your family have a child safety file shelter?

14. Flipped Safety Filer

On the website for the law firm of Quinn & Dworakowski, they guide children's parents through what they call "The Divorce Threat List." Elevated risk levels of verbal conflicts that either adult party involved in an open divorce case will undoubtedly declare on the other adult party. Psychological warfare tactics and operations, they warn, which are dangerous and unpredictable. This is expected. In the olden days of divorce wars, parties used parental disengagements for all sorts of weaponized and dirty things. These days families have been using an SPN to protect their families, relationships, investments, and security.

If Judith Willerstein were alive today, then we couldn't help but wonder if she would be a proponent or an opponent of joint family abilities – disconnecting and reconnecting at the same time. Would she support or oppose childproof contracts, a childproof safety file network, and a childproof community? Would she be for or against legislative initiatives that are both combative and cooperative? Could her children be shielded while embattling adults have their ways? Would she be for or against classical family law and Family Law 2.0 markets, each co-existing?

If Wallerstein had been kept out of her children's lives because she didn't fit a protocol, or because she had to serve two battling opponents instead of the children, then would we as a society be moving back in time or advancing? Could children of embattled adults ever have the light of day and a clean voice? What if childhood safety in policy was expected?

In conclusion, family unity and togetherness, highly outlawed and unfavored, is unexpected. Future research is needed and might include children in situations where dual restrictive parents are beyond legal or public remedy. Studies might consist of children of contracts and mechanisms with and without built-in remedies. Updates like a child safety seat during an automobile accident, child safety files before, during, and after a life wreck could be studied. Future studies might also include the number of houses children lose due to the absence of counsel when their parents are poor, and the quality of life associated with those experiences. Studies might also include the quantity of lost parental careers due to the absence of bail when accusations are made, and the resulting quality of life from those situations. Further studies may include the number of children whose parents lose educations, retirement accounts, and other such losses in gaps and the corresponding qualities of lives as a result. Many missing pieces themselves that escalate divorce conflicts like agents of pain with no equal healing agents of relief. After all, children don't choose the painful valleys of disengagements; our valleys choose them.

15. Bitfile

SAFETY FILERS: A Root & Peer-to-Peer Network

Abstract.

Clean safety files are your family's only organic, decentralized, peer-to-peer, safer private network (SPN). A solution that is a shelter for families of the problems with the multiple-hurting gaps in conventional "family" law & policy. Especially for these children who are inherently involved with increased number and intensities of multiple-hurting gaps.

Introduction

Society has come to rely almost exclusively on conventional "family" law and policy institutions serving as trusted third and fourth parties to process information, ideas, and issues. And while conventional "family" law practitioners work well enough for most cases, it still suffers from inherent voids that weaken its trust-based model. Completely non-reversible decisions and those consequences are not possible since law and policy institutions cannot avoid lag-time filings, lag-time hearings, and lag-time "solutions" to pre-pre-previous problems. Families must be aware of their authentic information in real-time. The cost, mechanisms, and lag-time insecurities may be greater at the ground level for survival rather than at various institutional position levels.

What is warranted for safety is the purely peer-to-peer version of filing familyhood positivity in real-time based on achievement proofs instead of systemic trust, that allows justice to be fair and balanced directly from the source of one parent to another without going through third, fourth, fifth, sixth, or seventh institutions. Allowing any two willing parties and/or peers to transact information directly with each other without the need for trusted external parties. Transactions that are personal and impractical to reverse would protect children from fraud, irreversible negative decisions, and corresponding time-lags.

Transactions

Clean Law defines a Clean Coin as the authentic relay of inner-family exchanges from positive parental actions and/or positive childhood achievements as defined directly by inner-family and friends. Each owner transfers coinage to the next by sharing informational transactions. (See Clean Law's "5 Coin Plan" framework for pay interactions). A payor or payee can verify the chain of positivity for the authenticity of ownership through the Clean Law network.

Timestamped Deals

Timestamped social media and/or surveys, acting as part of each safety file, is a solution proposed. In conventional family law and policy, written instruments enter those systems via "file stamp." Where all future actions revert back to this time and date. Which itself creates what's known as "lag-time" decisions after the facts.

A timestamp safety file works by visualizing a #hashtag folder of items each timestamped and widely publishing the #hashtag, such as on social media accounts, newspapers, or between peers. The timestamp proves that the data must have existed at the time, obviously, in order to get into the #hashtag file. Each timestamp includes the previous timestamp in its hash, forming an authentic and non-lag-able chain, with each additional timestamp reinforcing the ones before it. On a personal level, supporting the positive psychology sustainability of people.

Incentives

During each safety file transaction, a short follow-up survey is triggered with the offer of paying an additional Clean Coin (see Clean Coin Exchange) for completing the survey. This adds a digital version of safety file from survey completions on top of physical safety file versions

The incentive can also be funded with digital transaction fees and physical transactions. The incentive can also be funded by exchanging U.S. Currency for Clean Coinage such as a rate of $1 equaling 1 Clean Coin.

During authentic exchanges, a Clean Coin message bot would be on call with a digital survey within every transaction to earn an additional digital Clean Coin. The correspondence, for example, should read:

"How happy were you with your family's safety file experience? Please use the scale 1 (not at all satisfied) to 5 (extremely satisfied).

"How would you rate your satisfaction with the peer you networked with during the session? Please use the scale 0 (not at all satisfied) to 10 (extremely satisfied).

"Based on your experience with Clean Coin today, how likely are you to recommend it to another family member or friend? Please use the scale 0 (not at all satisfied) to 10 (extremely satisfied).

"Is there any additional feedback about your experience during the session you'd like to share?

"Thanks for your time.

Safety files can be easily absorbed into the SPN using the hashtag #safetyfile and other similar automatically sharable codes. Once absorbed, then the survey, payment, and account details can be automatically maintained.

Likewise, the physical account can be organically maintained or gauged approximately at any time to said digital account.

The incentive may help encourage honesty and balance. If a greedy attacker is able to assemble more digital exchanges than all the honest users, they would have to choose between using it to defraud themselves and their loved ones but not being able to "stealing up" the digital version, or being able to use the physical version to generate new digital coins.

They would find it absolutely profitable to play by the rules, such rules that favor them and their loved ones with potentially more new coins with every new healthy interaction.

Privacy

The conventional filing model achieves a level of privacy by labeling parties involved and the trusted third party as in "minor," "plaintiff," defendant," Attorney." The necessity to announce all transactions publicly precludes this method, but privacy can still be maintained by stacking the flow of information in another personal place: by keeping public users anonymous and unlisted. The public can see that someone is transacting to someone else, but without information linking the third party transaction to anyone. This is similar to the level of information released to the media and public through conventional filings, where the file stamp and charge of individual actions, is made public, but without telling who the filed parties are. As an additional firewall, no records outside of numerical data should be used for each digital incentive linked to a common owner. Some linking is still unavoidable with multi-input transactions, which necessarily reveal that their inputs were owned by the same owner. The risk is that if the owner of a file is revealed, linking could reveal other transactions that belonged to the same owner. But even so, in most cases of achievements recorded, revelations are believed to be wanted.

Cleaning Conclusions

Today consumers can get a 360-degree virtual tour of almost any apartment or street in the world. Yet many parents cannot see their child legally while everyone else in the world can. Why can't children see (at least virtually and rewardingly) their parents and family members?

We have proposed a system for electronic and physical transactions without relying on trust of conventional systems. Conventional family law and policy are like an Amtrak train, a subway car, or a bus. You buy the ticket first when you don't need it, and then you're subject to an old-fitting route, to all the stops, and all the detours alike. Never once being made aware of the lag-time incentives holding you and your family back at best, or to other routes at worse.

But our natural "child safety file" network is different. It's like a chartered limousine ride for your very precious children and family from the grassroots of your family to anywhere they want to go. This means that throughout the entire route of lives involved, all the stops, and all the detours, they can be ready for them. And the children are in a custom safety shelter. With authentic transactions, This is what can now get passed on to politician after politician. Not the filthy jankiness.

The network and Clean Coin Exchange are something lawyers can't see or do. It's something no city council can do. No county board, no state general assembly, and federal department can get it from indirect sources. A 360-virtual showcase of prized relationships in life! Not from a ratcheting "adult fighting file" (two-sided) perspectives. But from easy "child safety file" (authentic) perspectives. Enjoy your new life!

#practicesmall
@savinglives
//familysustainability

Unlike our competitors, Clean Law wants every child to have a family.

The ABCs of Clean Law's hope & encouragement fountain:
A - Families live safest when filing "A"lone.
B - Their most hopeful future is "B"ack-to-back on their own.
C - Peer-to-peer "C"ollaborations along the way are easy and fun, plus adds value and improved authentic performances.

We can all do a side of bifiling!

#enrichitforward
#americanfamily
#professionalclass

Anyone today and tomorrow should be able to go from ever darkening re-re-re-re-re-redacted papers into open access, understanding, inclusion and inherent family sustainability. It's our right and responsibility. Phenomenal new organic childhood, family and community re-developments.

Divisional problems?

Deployment war to children?

High-conflict divorce battle?

58

Toxic/hostile separation?

Stacked divisional problems?

Circuit clerk filings?

Court collesium?

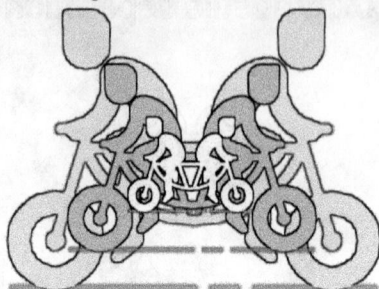

County board caucuses?

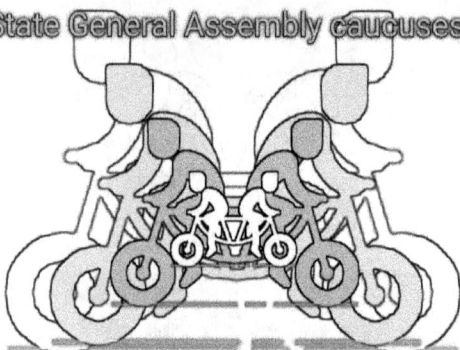

State General Assembly caucuses?

Side-Law & Side-Law – 360° Solutions

360-Degree solutions/Savings

cleanlaw.today
"Better future tomorrow"

"Open Access Peace-keeping that pays"

16. What's the Secret Sauce?

What's the secret with side-law?

Clean Law is happiness ☺ and healing ♥ - Sad ☹ social and digital stress & anxiety ✂ relief. Because a lot of people experience broken deals with broken trust. But Clean Law is like a comfort dog with a custom mission.

Have you ever subscribed to an app on your smartphone because it promised you the world and had a money-back guarantee so there was supposedly no way it could "get ya'"? Only to find out later, after you paid the price for a few months, that there was really nothing in it that you could use. And when you called customer service or tried to get help unsubscribing from the thing, you found out that there's no real customer service. Just a machine with loops and loops of recordings but no way to unsubscribe? That's a sad broken deal. And sometimes that's a sad broken heart.

How does Clean Law heal broken deals and broken hearts?

Well, first, it doesn't break them worse, but let's look at a couple of scenarios to explain it. A boy whose nickname was Ace has a puppy named Freedom. And as the puppy grows up, it sees and hears apps calling that says, "Come here for freedom!" And of course, Freedom goes. And some apps say, "Go there for freedom!" And of course, the puppy goes. But pretty soon, Freedom is all twisted up and turned around entangled in the divisiveness of life. Ever feel like that with your subscriptions? Leaving Freedom all strung out with a broken heart and broken deals like most of us.

Needless to say, Freedom got lost and parted ways from Ace. In the end, after all the deals were made, and no agreements kept Freedom on course, it read on the final gravestone, "The only place that I could NEVER return again was back to my roots." R.I.P Freedom.

How does Clean Law change the ending?

Now, there was another boy whose nickname was Crush and he had a puppy named Independence. And Crush had a heart for soldiers. So, he spent years and years raising and training Independence to be a comfort dog to hopefully give away to some lucky soldier. Crush trained Independence to pick up objects off the ground and to wake people up from sleep if they started to have nightmares. Crush eventually wanted to donate Independence to a wounded veteran who was trying to cope with PTSD or in a wheelchair with mobility issues.

But that charity endeavor for Crush turned sad and disheartening. Because as the puppy grew up it heard loud and adulterating signals like "Come to this app if you want independence." And like, "Go that way if you want something better!" Pretty soon, all pets like Independence get tied up to seemingly irresistible deals. To "This deal" or "That deal" but never to their real organic deal. Clean Law is clarity because the "tunnel vision" is one organic sustainability versus inorganic unsustainability. And at the destination, you'll see the differences between agreements with and without it. Broken hearts and broken agreements healed or just broke without it.

Did you know that without Clean Law, our lives with broken deals and broken hearts take us everywhere and anywhere except our roots - except where we were always expected to go?

On the flip side of life being turned inside-out, you probably know what it's like to see an airplane take off from the runway and then eventually reach its destination successfully? Airplanes don't just go haphazardly from start to finish. An airplane begins by taxiing towards the runway approaching takeoff. And you might be thinking, what if that was the deal that Freedom could have kept pace with?

When an airplane goes a little too far left or too far right off of course, then the control tower radios the pilots with corrections. And you might be thinking, what if our puppy dog never had to have life turned inside out and pinned to every app except its roots and its own successful destination?

If Freedom could deal happily and safely no matter what program it signed up with but had bad exit operations, then that would be a vital and successful workaround. That's Clean Law.

It's how to pivot the sadness and hostility into happiness and empathy.

What if Crush could have given Independence the life they had hoped for? What if the puppy could have had a protected heart through life and safer deals that they both deserved? Would the final tombstone say something different, maybe something about their roots and dreams?

All that being said, if you want to deal sad and dangerous like a misguided airplane, then keep choosing 180-degree situations.

But if you want to deal happy and safe like airplane pilots nudging you towards a successful destination, then choose 360-degree solutions like Clean Law provides.

And then whenever the app, product, or service you sign up for promises to be an excellent product with all the customer service in the world and a money-back guarantee, then we prevent a stubbed toe and automatic heal those deals if you do. It works for preventing crime and broken hearts too.

Deal happy and safe, not sad and dangerous.

Since the discovery of side-law, many university programs now have Integrative Studies being offered including Michigan State University and Southern Illinois University Edwardsville. When conducting cross disciplinary research, however, it's important to identify areas in both fields that are directly comparable, thus helping knowledge transfer (Howard and Dekoninck, 2008). The research in this integrative study to finally discover the secret spans psychology and engineering. So it's important to identify a specific areas in both that lends a hand to the new transfer knowledge (Howard and Dekoninck, 2008).

Researchers wanted to describe the creative design process by the integration of engineering design and psychology literature (Howard and Dekoninck, 2008). It was felt that taking elements from types of designs proposed in engineering design and the meaningful results proposed in psychology would produce a modern consensus view of both (Howard and Dekoninck, 2008). A blend that could further link new types of creative designs for industry.

To conduct this cross-disciplinary investigation, researchers first found areas in both engineering design and psychology literature that are directly comparable, thus making knowledge transferable (Howard and Dekoninck, 2008). Researchers saw that in psychology, it's common to refer to creativity in terms of three primary areas by which are studied, namely the creative "process," the creative "product (output)," and the creative "environment." (Howard & Dekoninck, 2008; Murdock & Puccio,1993; Basadur et al., 2000). In engineering design, they saw four broadly similar sections, namely the design "problem," the design "process," the design "type" (output), and the design "activity" (Howard and Dekoninck, 2008; Ullman, 2010; Cross, 2008).

Researchers proposed a "creative design process" from spanning engineering and psychology (Howard and Dekoninck, 2008). A composite of three reformulated "design output operations" are presented. Which are believed to transfer elements from the different design types from engineering design and the creative outputs offered in psychology. One new operation is called the original design output. It's defined as a design output in which there is a creative output at the behavioral level. A second new operation is called the adaptive design output. It's defines as a design output in which there is a creative output and the functional level. And a third operation is called the variant design output. It's defined as a design output in which there is a creative output and the structural level.

These new definitions also mean a coherent way to measure elements and gauge any solutions proposed for effectiveness of and community synchronization or industry impacts. Future research must be conducted in more detail to build up these findings from integrative studies programs. It was proposed that the "obviousness" and the "source" of information are essential to effectively integrate disciplines (Howard and Dekoninck, 2008).

Since gatekeeping is the creative operation, then connection-keeping is hypothesized to be the design portion of that pen. In theory, this review of gatekeeping and connection-keeping should in practice measure the elements of obstructive gates and gauge the effectiveness of various types of relief bridges and those impacts on the market or community well-being

17. Engineered Design

Since the beginning of the Information Age, demonstrating links between systemic functions associated with human beings of all ages have received increased attention by academic researchers and market researchers alike. Once customer discovery for a new industry design has been completed, then that new design can be engineered (Yoon, 2009). Although there are many views on what exactly is engineered design and the engineering design process, a running example throughout the rest of this paper should help clear things.

18. Pre-Design Thinking

Market research often incorporates participatory design, which involves end-users in design-thinking (Davidson & Jensen, 2013). In one study, Microsoft Research wanted to discover how the root users of smartphone application ages 4-6 might co-design an app to help these preschoolers plan their playtime during the day. Previous studies had shown that few co-design methods exist for children under the age of six. They also wanted to understand the effectiveness of co-designs for end-users ages 4-6 and younger preschoolers.

Very young children are known consumers of digital media. In fact, 97% of infants are using a smartphone before their first birthday and 75% of children own a dedicated mobile device by the time they turn four (Hiniker et al., 2005). In the pre-designing phase of developing an app, scientists must realize how end-users can function so that the final product is viable before it's design is funded. Designing for this class of customer's needs, interests, and social attachments are different than designing for adult users (Hiniker et al., 2005).

Researches conducted a two-hour co-design workshop with seven children age 4-6. They used established participatory design techniques, including comicboarding, a construction activity, and traditional user testing to elicit design ideas. The comicboard, or storyboard, was presented in a way so that children could help fill in a final empty frame where the previous two frames guided planning a birthday party for R2D2. It was discovered ahead of time with conversations with parents that all of the co-designers could relate to a Star Wars theme. In the first frame, a facilitator read what was drawn - a conversation between a child and C-3PO talking about planning the party for R2D2. In the second scene, C-3PO asked the child how to show what he thinks should be planned first. And in the third blank scene, children were then instructed to draw what they think should be in the next scene (Hiniker et al., 2005).

It was discovered that researchers could easily elicit on-topic designs from 5- and 6-year-old preschoolers. For example, one child drew a scene of planning to take pictures at the party. However, exchanges with 4-year-old participants broke down, and children struggled to articulate a thought for action. For example, one child suggested "Big circles" should be in the next scene of planning a birthday party for R2D2 (Hiniker et al., 2005).

Researchers found that 5- and 6-year-old co-designers were able articulate their work so that designers could easily understand and build the ideas. While 4-year-olds created less cohesive ideas and often deflected to other topics. It was also thought that 4-year-olds should have been asked more about what they meant to understand better. Further studies were suggested to include 4-year-olds in the scope of their design. Thus, giving them scaffolding, or an equal voice. After all, they are the experts at being children (Hiniker et al., 2005).

In this age of information, child-computer interactions have come to increasingly value children in the pre-design process (Hiniker et al., 2005). This means that a responsive self-reporting element should be considered in the pre-design phase of all age-appropriate device designs. A well-planned pre-design component for products and services that authentically involve children could also have the potential to reduce potentially frustrating barriers and also assist academic preparedness.

19. Elementary Engineering Design

Researchers examined high school student perceptions of the engineering design process because educators and policymakers agree that engineering content must be part of K-12 classrooms (Berland et al., 2014). This agreement is evident, researchers suggest, to meet twenty-first century needs. Studies show a trend in the availability of engineering in K-12 curricula, according to Katehi (2009), and national policy documents argue that inclusion of engineering into K-12 classrooms will soon be the norm (National Research Council, 2012).

In this study, researchers explored ways in which participating in design supports or inhibits the student's association with math, science, and engineering (Berland et al., 2014). They also analyzed ways in which participating in design supports or inhibits the association with applying math and science knowledge and engaging in engineering practices (Berland et al., 2014).

Researchers first defined the engineering design process (EDP). They found that there is no single EDP. The procedures differ by industry, experiences, and projects in the work of professional engineers (Berland et al., 2014). Even with those variations, the educational community has recognized core characteristics of the EDP, including (1) the EDP begins with a problem clearly defined; (2) practitioners find custom approaches to choosing between many possible solutions; and (3) the design (noun) requires assessment and analysis (Berland et al., 2014).

Previous research demonstrates that engaging in the act of design supports students in representing math, science, and engineering content as well as increasing student motivation, ownership, and engagement (Berland et al., 2014). This finding corroborates previous research that found the positive impact of design activities in learning environments (Berland et al., 2014).

By the end of the project, these studies suggest the EDP and context should include a reason for K-12 students to go beyond design and engage in the harder work of integrating math and science into the approach of their plans. Educators, it was theorized, must develop engineering design challenges where students are unable to succeed without practicing the quantitative math and science aspects of the work (Berland et al., 2014). This means that graduated challenge and reward levels would more effectively design mobile apps for end-users. For example, a pre-school "Connection-Keeper" journaling app might challenge and reward differently than a high school "Connection-Keeper" journaling app.

Bright & Brighter

20. The Connection-Keeping Process

Researchers indicate that the engineering design process (EDP) can be thought of at different developmental stages for clarity. The Museum of Science Boston, for example, has a program called "Engineering is Elementary" where students in grades 1 through 5 can learn the engineering design process to "Improve Play Dough." While in 1712 Thomas Newcomen saw a need to pump the water from the bottom of coal mines and used the process to design the first steam engine (Plan & Khandani, 2005).

An early area for both from disciples this study can be thought of as children's physical and virtual connections with their separated parents, or their mutual parental attachments. Studies show that when children design an improved Play Dough, they often thought in terms of colors, physical characterstsics, and pulling apart and putting back together in a relatively new fashion (Plan & Khandani, 2005).

This means that if kids reimagine connection-keeper (CK), for example, they would see their parents in terms of physical characteristics, and perhaps pulling them apart and putting them back together. However, children with a healthy number and healthy quality attachments may ot see the need to improve their Play Dough like those children with unhealthy Play Dough. For example, immediately delivering a phone call from one parent to the child may not seem as necessary for children who have experienced healthy attachments as with those who have experienced unhealthy "attachments."

Connection-keeping views, therefore, would be different than gatekeeping views in a sense that as a case progresses in terms of depths of conflict, all the way up until a judge has to decide one way or the other, then corresponding bonds or lack of bonds would progress as well, and the quantity of connections/disconnections would accumulate, but the mold presser may not know or believe a need to reimagine Play Dough. Thus, according to research, this means that fulfilling the best long-term adjustment of children within the gaps of escalating conflicts and within the gaps of knowledge may also very be a practice in futility (Wemple, 2020).

21. Connection-Keeping Products

Khandani (2005) studied an educational transfer plan for use in a design course in engineering intending to provide hands-on experience for people interested in engineering. Researchers felt that by observing our surroundings, we see examples of creativity and emerging technology everywhere. Physical objects like mobile phones, drones, and smart vehicles all coming into being through a creative process.

In the psychology portion of this paper, research showed the typology of gatekeeping. Now in the engineering portion, studies show types of connection-keepings. For example, an engineer doesn't usually build a product for the market without first carefully pre-designing it to fit end-users. Thus, filtering a "best-fit" solution for customers to a problem. A necessary design process includes defining the relevant problem, gathering pertinent information, generating multiple solutions, testing, and implementing a final solution (Khandani, 2005). The design process is especially crucial for the safety of those who physically construct the product, such as a new bridge, and for those who finally use the product like automobile drivers (Behm, 2005).

Studies show that the second phase of basic design is to collect information that relates to the problem (Khandani, 2005). For example, virtual mobile apps are one possibility for children in the middle of a divorce to collaborate with their parents (Hiniker et al., 2005). And then there are other ways like through teachers, phones, mail, events, and public promotions that children can share cooperative attachments with their parents.

According to Appadvice (2019), one mobile app that has recently come to market is called the Custody Transfer Log. This app virtually discovers evidence from both the quantity and the quality of first-party connections between children and their parents during physical visitation exchanges. Evidence of these interactions between children and both of their parents can be easily entered onto a mobile device, compiled, saved, and even printed for court. Professor Musonda Kapatmoyo is the co-founder of the Custody Transfer Log app says that thousands of people are using such connection-keeping apps themselves following divorce.

This study means that pre-designing other products like a mobile app for better protection of children's telephone exchanges with their parents could be a final product (Khandani, 2005). Gaps in connection-keeping designs and corresponding research may also include other products to keep connections, include a phone exchange app, mail exchange app, school calendar exchange app, sporting event exchange app, religious exchange app, a helpful "How-to" app, a "show and tell" app, a social media exchange app, and even virtual holographic visitations. Deep-level, machine learning, and artificial intelligence that could theoretically be real-time micro-justice for all no matter what.

Before attempting a motorized flight, the Wright brother first made more than 700 successful glider flights (Buede, 2002). The Custody Transfer Log is an example of a product which has been test and implemented as a final solution to a problem. A design process for better protection of children's physical exchanges with their parents. This means that children who are involved with a HC divorce may not be able to pre-test their resulting life, but there are self-reporting tools which could begin preparing them for being in mechanically grounded middle.

From psychology research, studies have proven that most parents are cooperative (Austin et al., 2013), and judges can assess parents and caseworkers on specific open-gate and closed-gate behaviors (Austin, Pruett, et al., 2013). This means that parents and policymakers can likewise virtually initiate connection-keeping information, which could hypothetically be a design component of a mobile app suite that automatically sends digital data to a public or private database for reference. However, a gap exists in the availability of a suite of compatible self-reporting tools.

22. Designing the Pain Squad App

In a Canadian hospital for children with cancer, researchers planned to design a gamified mobile app for patients to function as a real-time electronic pain diary (Stinson et al., 2013). Researchers believe that proper assessments are the essential first step to manage pain effectively and that paper-based approaches involving patient recall lead to inaccuracies and biases in the reporting of events. There is no well-validated self-assessing tool to evaluate sensory (intensity, quality, and location of pain) and affect (emotional effects). Designing and developing an electronic-based mobile app to assess and capture pain events as they occur was thought to represent a superior method of treatment (Stinson et al., 2013). The objective of this study was to design, develop, and then test the feasibility, usability, and compliance of a game-based smartphone pain assessment tool for adolescents with cancer.

Researchers first developed pain assessment questions using the e-Ouch electronic juvenile arthritis pain diary as a template. They then generated low-fidelity pre-designs of the proposed app and looked to understand the qualitative usability and navigational structure. Audio-taped interviews and interactive videos of congratulatory effects from police officers were studied. Patients would role-play as detectives investigating pain and have their rank increased with the consistency of use.

Once the pre-design elements were studied and iterated, then a capital investment was made to create a prototype. Once the app was functional, compliance data was collected from a 2-week feasibility trial where users were alarmed to record their pain twice a day, morning, and evening (Stinson et al., 2013).

(Source: www.jmir.org/2013/3/e51, 2013)

The app was programmed to be accessible using an iPhone 4S. Its design was a client-server architecture, where the client-side was built in native Apple iOs code to manage incoming pain assessments. A website interface with password protection was incorporated to allow researchers to add new participants and access results. Assessment information was transferred to a server using an encrypted protocol whenever the app was online (Stinson et al., 2013).

Studies showed that adolescents with cancer had difficulty relating to a typical game theme for the app and indicated the need to iterate the theme to improve desirability. To redress this issue, the theme was changed to "Pain Squad." Similarly, a designed product included an initial "body map" (left) and an updated body map (right). Another change was an initial pain scale (lower left) and an updated frame (lower right side). End-users advised that on the original "body map" they couldn't clearly understand the parts of the body on the image. And that the wording and lack of numbers on the initial pain scale were confusing (Stinson et al., 2013).

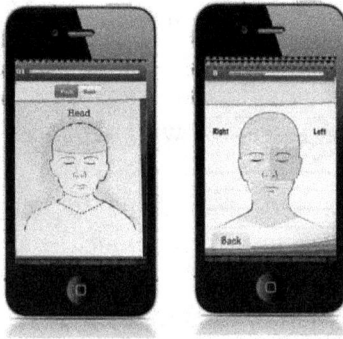

(Source: www.imir.org/2013/3/e51, 2013)

Before   After

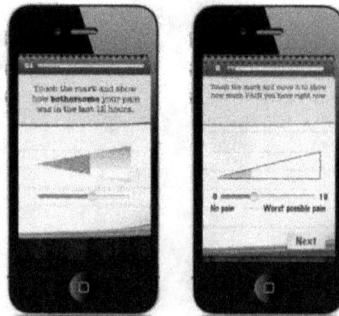

(Source: www.imir.org/2013/3/e51, 2013)

Before   After

The results of this study mean that game-based mobile apps to address real-time pain in children is feasible and clinically helpful (Stinson et al., 2013). Researchers also established that the content validity of a pain assessment questioner through question-importance ratings by end-users. Gamified health information tools using iPhones improve compliance with reporting. Researchers found that adolescents with cancer enjoyed using the app over two weeks, found it to be attractive, and the rewards component while role-playing effective (Stinson et al., 2013).

23. Connection-Keeping Environments

Theoretically, cooperative co-parenting (CC) may never reach the point where a judge must make a decision based upon state factors that are believed to be in the best interest of the child. For example, a patient can never get help with pain unless he interacts with a doctor. Divorce and conflicts may reach the severity where a judge must make a decision. Still, by then, any cooperative evidence is outside the scope of a trial, and both sides must gear for battle while strategically discrediting their opponent. Court is well-known to be psychological warfare.

Connection-keeping, in the parallel market, is inherently ground-level. Real-time activities that aren't always inclusive with the circuit clerks where motions and counter motions are filed. Actions and abilities which are not taught as acceptable in classical law schools, nor any schools for that matter. This is a significant gap that raises a red flag for the nearly 50% of our children in society who have no voice if and when a conflict in their family culminates beyond common remedies. What if the system fails all three – the statutory gatekeepers, the benevolent connection-keepers, and the vulnerable blank spots in the middle?

24. A Safer VPN Protocol from Life Hackers

In an interview between Hosts Jessy Katz and Johny Caplan along with CEO Amit Baraket, the founder of Safer VPN (virtual private network), on the business startup show Tech Talk, it was explained very well about who modern day security experts are, and why they do what they do to co-protect the public Lansford (2019).

Johny Caplan asked CEO Amit Baraket to tell viewers who were watching Tech Talk to explain his company Safer VPN and why they put it together. Amit explains that Safer VPN is a team of cyber security experts put together to deliver safer privacy on the internet for the public.

Host Johny Caplan goes on to say that a VPN is like a tunnel that users can use to shield their information while navigating the internet privately. It masks your internet connection to make it appear like you're somewhere else. In the old days, Johny says, people used to use it for all kinds of dodgy things they did on the internet. But these days people use it just to protect their privacy, property, and to gain access to places where they might be overruled and excluded like mad dictatorships Lansford (2019).

CEO Baraket goes on to share that by utilizing a VPN, you have a private tunnel where no one can see what you do and protect your assets anonymously. When users expose themselves using public wi-fi networks, they are in danger of being hacked if they don't use a VPN. It only takes a couple of seconds for someone to steel your information and property.

In engineering designs, a cornerstone case is thought to be a situation or a problem that occurs only outside of the normal operating parameters – specifically one that transforms itself when multiple environmental conditions are simultaneously at extremes, even though each condition may be within a specified range for the parameters (Compton et al. 1991). Researchers say that in the past, enterprises would install internet lines across long distances to ensure secured data transfer. Those were cornerstone cases that demanded inclusion from the sender and receiver because information, or lack thereof, is valuable. However, those connections were impractical and not always feasible, so the most recent solution to this problem is what's known as a virtual private network (VPN) (Jaha, 2020).

A virtual VPN is a way to provide private communications between members of a group using public communication lines. There are many different VPN solutions, so researchers wanted to categorize them as trusted VPNs, client-based VPNs, and provider-based VPNs (Jaha, 2020). This study was essential to help network engineers decide which VPN solution might be best for their project.

Researchers looked at various VPNs to serve as a basis for creating a wide area network that allows the resources of a company to be remotely accessed (Jaha, 2020). VPNs give enterprises the same capabilities as a private physical line, but with increased access capabilities and a much lower cost. Researchers looked at various architectural designs and categorized solutions accordingly (Jaha, 2020).

Studies showed that trusted VPNs are paths that are leased from service providers, and that the architecture and protocols of a company's local area network (LAN) have to match the architecture and protocols of the service provider's wide area network (WAN) (Jaha, 2020).

Client-based VPNs are often used with remote users. Client-based, or web-based, VPNs are considered the standard technology. This solution typically reduces the cost associated with corresponding software but can also complement the more expensive trusted VPN use (Jaha, 2020).

Research shows that outsourced provider-based VPNs reduce the in-house skills needed and reduces a company's security labor costs. It also gives a predictable cost. However, the company's that outsource provider-based VPNs lose control over their VPN security and the number of remote users (Jaha, 2020).

Secure VPNs are developed using encryption and other security mechanisms like integrity checking and authentication. The traffic is shielded at one network edge or sending computer, before passing through the communication lines, and then unshielded when it reaches the company's local network or receiving equipment. Trusted VPNs are more intensive and consist of one or more paths leased from a service provider. Client-based VPNs are the most common but usually require additional staff and software maintenance. While client-based, or web-based, VPNs are more financially feasible but have more restrictive components (Jaha, 2020).

25. The Clean Law SPN

Where is the mystery in adult parents being caught-up in military deployments or divorce?

Where's the secret spot in keeping children's parents apart from each other?

In the meteorology world, a tornado "outbreak" is an event where multiple tornadoes spawn out of the same weather system. The number of tornadoes required to qualify as an outbreak typically are at least six to ten according to the Weather Service.

In the family sustainability world for children who are caught in the middle of legal divisive protocols like divorce, or literal "eye of the storm," they can experience a similar occurrences like a tornado outbreak. We now define these family unsustainability outbreaks as the occurrence of multiple contract-making protocols spawned by the same escalating legal practices. The number of upheavals required to qualify as a "contrado" (contract dispute plus tornado) outbreak are one to four according to Clean Law.

But, unfortunately, instead of a tornado outbreak close to each other but in different locations, family unsustainability outbreaks are like several different tornadoes breaking out all in one unprotected spot - the children. Which feels like blue on top of black, a hammer on an anvil, a prickly experience on top of a prickly experience, scared of being hit on top of scared.

The parents of these children are logically the only ones who are in a unique position to shield them from any outbreak of upheavals. And a decentralized peer-to-peer network of parents can also psychology support one another and be even safer for the children of outbreaks. But there were no previous warning systems in place. So, child safety files, family sustainability, the U.S. Family Unsustainability Rating Scale, and organic family law and policy practices were born.

Have you ever heard of the child safety file?

The **solution** is just like an encouraging comfort pet for children who are innocently involved with deployment, divorce, parental separation, or other paper dispute, and piece of mind for their parents. Half of which, are generally innocent in the divergent hostility themselves.

The solution keeps America's vulnerable population safer. Especially during lethal trying times.

Phenomenal
new child,
family, and
community
advancements.

At the
intersection
of
misery and relief.

Now with a side
of healing...

www.cleanlaw.today

A safer private
network (SPN).

26. Organic Family Law 2.0 Validated

Introducing side-law. The CLEAN CLEAN CLEAN way of life which includes virtual and physical child safety files, family sustainability data, and a safer private network (SPN) of organic probabilities. Because research shows that conventional "family" law v. law like policy v. policy creates inherent gaps in knowledge, understanding, and physically risky situations. They literally create re-re-re-re-redacted people. Law's "adult fighting files" with uncommon legal instruments, third party entry gates, and situational decisions literally implies nothing but blind spots, or stacked blind spots, for every innocent man, woman and child involved. Leaving these intellectual and then physical gaps open and throbbing leaving us all at risk (Wemple, 2018).

Don't forget the safety files!

In the study of Family Law 2.0, research shows what's called the top 10 gaps in classical family law and its filing system. One blank spot is the "Versus Void." In other words, in divorce case titles such as "Jane Doe vs. John Doe," the device "versus" voids out a place in those entitling deals where children like "Junior Doe" could be. Junior, in that case, is no longer highly seen as existing while his or her parents are highly seen as strict adversaries. Other gaps where children could be are the Table-less Void, the gap between the two tables in the courtroom. The No Voice Void, and the Party-less Gap (as in Plaintiff, Defendant, etc.). In this study, the author wanted to design safety bridges for these valleys because on top of the absence of normal parental rights in court, it was believed that these additional gaps are dangerous for children to crawl through all alone (Wemple, 2018).

In contrast to divisive principles, research has also shown that the child safety file system includes a custom file folder for each child, golden paper clips, a table for the children, a chair for the child, a child's name written on the folder by themselves or by their parents, a voice, a pen or other documenting instrument, a permanent record of their positive achievements, and many other safety bridges. Practitioners can nominate a child for doing something great, like coping well through a separation. That charge can be heard, and then voted on to see if it should be placed in their permanent record or not. Traditionally, these trials have taken place in a community center set up like a board room where the child working on their file has a prominent seat at the table.

A classical grandfather move, besides asking their grandkids to pull their finger, is bending over and feeling junior's muscles and commenting on how they are developing. Grandfather might say with widening eyes, "Wow!" Or, he might shake his head and say, "Hmm… you may need to eat a little Spinach. The point is, collaborative divorce care shouldn't expect to understand any child of divorce by feeling someone else's muscle.

It's well-known that our own human bodies have this automatic shield which protects the pupil of our eyes, to protect the most sensitive part of our sight and body. Studies show that this authentic Family Law 2.0 with child safety files is like our eyelid, shielding the most sensitive part of our family during military deployments and divorce.

Studies show that the first 6-year-old girl named Madison, who practiced a safety file with her dad, called it "The best day of my life." The first two words that a second 6 year-girl named Alayna wrote in her file were "Love, love." Family Law 2.0 practitioners have also introduced innovative new county, state, and federal policy initiatives like the Clean Child support Initiative to reduce wrongful lag-time charges, Madison's Initiative to reduce the number of continuances, and the 2020 Family Bill – Sustaining our Future (Wemple, 2019).

This updated practice means that like your favorite smartphone, community family law can have newer and newer versions. Albeit, classical divorce contracts and traditional court mechanisms may not be the best suited for reducing childhood conflicts. For example, there often are no built-in remedies in divorce agreements when a child's mom or dad is injured in a car accident and then in a wheelchair for a year. And there is no automatic or reflective mechanisms to go back and adjust those terms according to reality unless a Modification is filed. Then new future terms can be reflected to that filing date. The difference between a real-time stop in pay due to an accident and the modification date filing is known as lag-time. And everyone knows that even lag-time on our computers can cause frustration. Can you imagine being charged for the time you are down? These children's parents go to jail when they can't comply with the lagging terms of concrete contracts and mechanisms regardless. Research shows that divorce agreements and those mechanisms without built-in fluid remedies can cannibalize childhood (Wemple, 2019). Research also shows that with Family Law 2.0, children can be relieved of this pain when the community works with them, publishes, and records their positive accomplishments through a safer private network (SPN).

Evidence shows that Clean Law's SPN is a growing peer-to-peer family of childhood safety experts linked together to support and encourage safer familyhood experiences while passing through public sectors (Wemple, 2018). Much like a VPN is a private network service delivered through a public network infrastructure (Bollapragada et al., 2005). The simplest way to think of a SPN is like two children smiling at each other or playing tag within a bigger angry community. One cannot imagine how impossible it is for children to stay in their parent's lives when one parent has a slave name like "non-custodial." Individuals alone often cannot access their children's school event dates, sporting event

93

dates, report cards, social media accounts, mail, phone, college plans, etc. "Custodial" v. "non-custodial" is a state of gates in-of-itself.

PROFESSIONAL

GRADE

INDUSTRIAL

STRENGTH

BATTLE ZONE

TESTED

EASILY ENRICH FAMILY VALUE

Don't forget the safety files!

Move forward together

Organic safety files change everything.

Research shows that one community is using a safer SPNs and shielding children of divorce through their divorce wars. Mississippi College of Law Professor Alena Ng Boyte, for example, calls Family Law 2.0 "An innovative new program mitigating the effects of divorce on children." Studies show that family members can now publish and record their SPN regardless of the level of conflict their parents and institutions establish as policy. And it is easier to do than operating a phone.

Organic family law, hence, community safety.

No "horse" and "buggy" attached!

New Skills, New Deals, New Economy

27. Five Reasons Safety Filers Can Charge More

A poll was taken at the Donald Danforth Plant Science Center in St. Louis, MO, and revealed that most Americans think organic family law isn't worth the cost because consumers believe organics are the same as conventional items, simply with a fancy organic label attached. In fact, initial participants were unsettled towards even the thought of organic family law. However, anyone can try organic child safety files themselves and see actual differences between organic family law/policy and conventional family law/policy. Even though many are private parents themselves, there are many genuine reasons why organic family law practitioners can and should be expensive.

Here are the top 5 reasons organic family law costs more.

1.Time Requirements

The price can be credited to time issues. Time is precious, and natural cultivators of family sustainability invest much more energy into their case files than conventional practitioners.

2. Innovation Demands

Since organic, or natural practitioners don't utilize the same paper instruments and the same mechanical placements of maneuvers on their opponents/vulnerable like conventional practices, they have to search for other, more innovative techniques and complementary instruments for situations to build their case files. These innovative skills keep organic practitioners moving forward; however, they do cost more.

3. Assessing Each Families Risks & Rewards

From practitioners to processors and decisionmakers, most confirmed family sustainability moves warrant a safer private network (SPN) for further developments. As well as a fitting work setting and equipment before creating organic law. All the while, networking to understand any hostile maneuvers that may be exercised against their vulnerabilities.

On top of new grounds, skills, and new economy, innovative activities are often on location to the point that they don't warrant a full office and conventional staff, which implies either finding a fluid collaboration area or using for digital data collectors like the Custody Transfer Log smartphone app for custom documentation.

Nearly half of the adult population in America experience just divorce, and almost everyone else has experienced separation. Many while having children – the true victims. But virtually no one reaches out to offer a lending hand to help children stay connected with both of their first loves – both of their parents. In fact, that is highly shunned. But today, one company and its practitioners are reaching out and lending hand to help keep all children connected to both of their first loves. Which is especially critical during the vital young years of their lives. People would be polluted and less than clean by not accepting this helping hand.

4. Education

When it comes to new organic knowledge, skills, and abilities, practitioners spend a significant amount of time and money for ongoing workshops, participation in community support, and pursuing continued education. And not just any education, but academics spanning multiple minor degree areas like engineering and psychology. A pivot from just one specific major like conventional law.

Conventional practices are also influenced by unfair financial allocations from the government, which do not go along with organic practices. In most cases, financial assignments are very explicitly geared towards diverging families unsustainably apart, not towards sustainability practices of keeping children connected. For example, many state court systems and individual courts (which organic family law is not a part of), take advantage of federal funding under Title IV-D of the Social Security Act to obtain reimbursements for the costs of contracting child support issues and negotiating conventional family law matters. In fact, a report by Authenticated U.S. Governmental Information, notes that between 2002 and 2006, American taxpayers spent over $44 trillion in allotments for conventional family law (Section 8-Child Support Enforcement Program, n.d.), with most of the allocations given to matters handled by persons and organizations other than "judges" per state statutes (Zorza et al., 2017). In other words, bags of money go along with classical case files, while no allocations of money go along with organic child safety files. These practitioners are simply "bootstrapping" it, and there are no protocols to include organic files at any table of decision. They're just for family support and not centralized outside support.

5. New Economy

Natural family law and policy are a brand-new economy that independent practitioners themselves are launching. Instead of just commonly mining for negativities like convention economies, this organic practice goes against multiple grains like a Salmon trying to swim up multiple streams and through numerous cascading waterfalls to mine for positivity. It's a very tough economy for new-school fish.

LICENSING & COUNSELING

MONUMENTAL

CUSTOMER SERVICE

28. Licensing & Counseling Training:

A Visual Guide to the Conventional "5 Dollar Drain"

Break-ups shouldn't happen every day. In fact, in a perfect world, we shouldn't feel the need to break-up with our loved ones at all. A major benefit of the peer-to-peer child safety file network is that it often prevents escalating break-up commentaries. In the event that you normally need to a break, try talking to another family and adding something a little different to your meals.

For the times that family's occasionally need to split, check out the options below, along with some common over-reaching mistakes that could warrant caution.

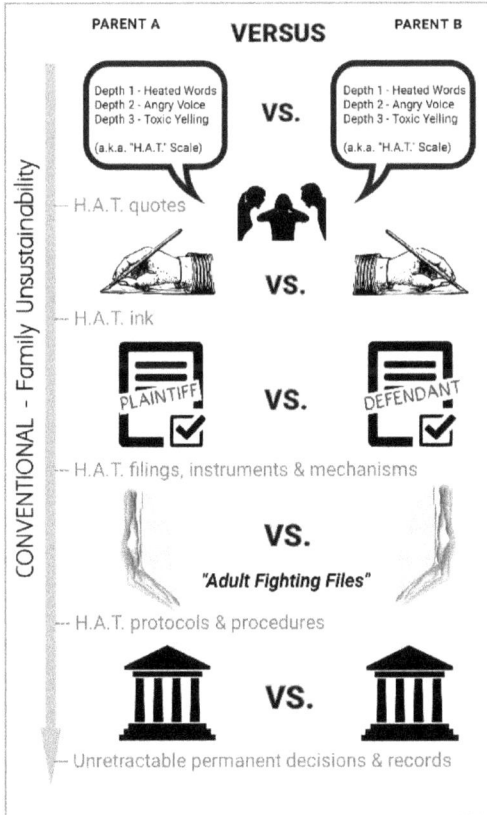

Or, for those who are more icon-oriented, introducing the FUAL Scale:

Divergent-Protocols-Based
Family Unsustainability Alert Levels (FUAL)

Null	Collaborate	Advisory	Watch	Warning
Blank	Red	Orange	Amber	Yellow

Increasing Levels of Risk ------------------->

But whether divergent ways are necessarily escalating beyond control or not, please check out the options below, along with some common under-served areas that deserve greater promotion in practice. Child safety files and organic Family Law 2.0 take advantage of the simple "Welcome to clarity" 5 Coin Plan of family sustainability regardless of conventional unsustainable protocols.

A Visual Guide to the Organic "5 Coin Plan"

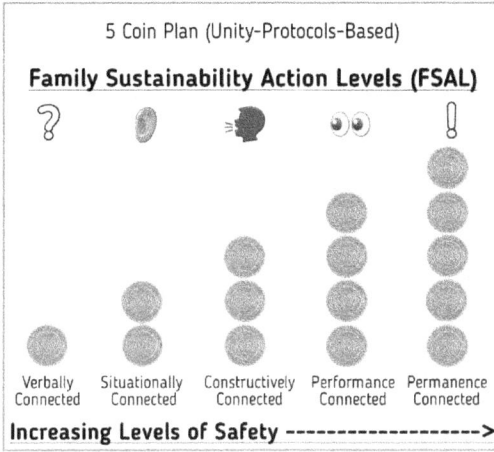

5 Coin Plan (Unity-Protocols-Based)

Family Sustainability Action Levels (FSAL)

| Verbally Connected | Situationally Connected | Constructively Connected | Performance Connected | Permanence Connected |

Increasing Levels of Safety ------------------->

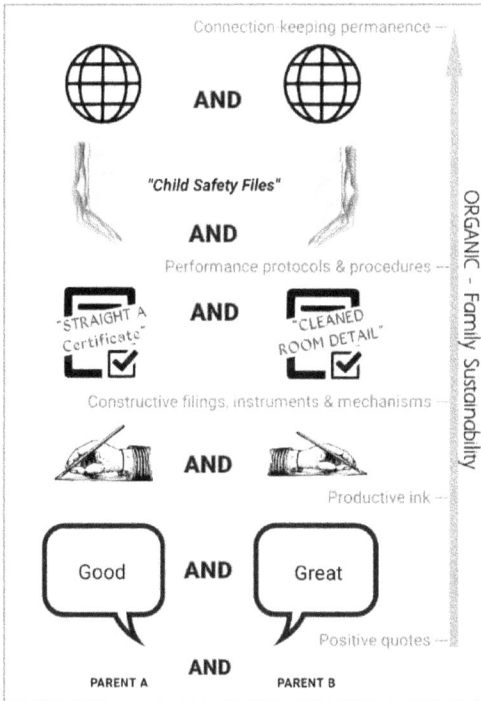

Connection-keeping permanence ---

AND

"Child Safety Files"

AND

Performance protocols & procedures ---

"STRAIGHT A Certificate" **AND** "CLEANED ROOM DETAIL"

Constructive filings, instruments & mechanisms ---

AND

Productive ink ---

Good **AND** Great

Positive quotes ---

AND

PARENT A   PARENT B

ORGANIC – Family Sustainability

29. MILESTONES - "Heroes at Law"

Who wins now? "WE DO - WE DO!"

Are you a veteran or through with deployment to war, and perhaps lost your PURPOSE of serving?

Like the Pony Express, the grounds on each side of those fast and furious horse riders may have been at times like a deconstructive and deadly force, but newfound victory may be one new transition away.

Are you divorced or separated and lost the PERMANENCE you thought you had with marriage?

Like many front-line heroes working on new cases and cleaning up toxic psychological messes, newfound protection may be one family away from you. Helping blend those unsustainable family situations into new sustainability situations and clarity of child safety files could be the difference between life and death - a great milestone forevermore!

Clean Coin Exchange (CCE) for Family & America

CCE

The sustainability reward program for family & America.

*A supportive peer-to-peer exchange helping
organic family law & policy co-exist.*

Stacked family hostility files/policies also have their own blank check currency. Back and forth positions like rocks unnecessarily taxing governments like "Republican" caucuses and "Democratic" caucuses at the county board meetings and state general assembly meetings. Both of these are like heavier and heavier rocks on the people. Especially children.

So, another authentic way to shield children, be a voice for family and save our community from hostile take-overs is through a separate currency. A family sustainability exchange called the Clean Coin exchange (CCE).

Every healthy and sustainable organization needs its own shareable, balanced currency. Or, balanced paperwork. From both the institution's perspective and from the user's perspective. It's common sense that people left out and in the middle but still subject to both sides are going to end up biased. A permanent record like armed guards forcing them down one trail is left like breads crumbs for a trial.

CCE competitors, politics, parties and police, can't even share their legal instruments authentically with the people they are about. Yet, they can spread their version of the story far and wide to the middle. These are armed guards making children go down a trail of permanently believing one intuitional side over the other on-institutional side. Quite possibly victims that can't be realized until decades on down the road. Even if then. In these world's, family sustainability stops. It's dead upon arrival at best. Painted ugly, published ugly, and buried forever that way at worst.

But upon entering the organic family law and policy world, childhood safety and family sustainability never end. They never come to the point where an attorney, judge, representative, or "Monday morning" policy must intervein. Especially since it now means a plethora organic childhood, family and community developments.

Move forward together

Don't forget the safety files!

Conventional ∞ Organic

30. How to Survive Hell's Motor with Heaven's Oil

A different kind of justice

Since the rise of deployment and divorce wars, the extremely complicated battle that exists within **family law systems is** escalate similar to modifying a V8 car engine. Where the people who are below the system of laws (namely, petitioner and respondent) would be the pistons or connecting rods, which absorb all the heat from the system, and the forgotten area would be the children, or crankshaft.

Now, if moms, dads and children in family cases want to avoid an overload of heat from the engine, then lawyers and concerned citizens can now offer *Clean Law SPN*, which is a kind of an extremely safe protective shield with fully refined motor oil, which contains a really innovative built-in cooling system that prevents damage to human parts. It's not only responsible for the protection and cooling of figurative connecting rods

111

and bearings, but also protecting, saving and recovering any damage in the crankshaft and powertrain of society. All this will avoid thermal breakdowns of our family, hence social vehicles.

LAW v. LAW

During up and down transitions, the area where the pistons, connecting rods, and bearings are located are outside the scope of the fuel inlet, outlet, and circulation of the consuming fire within the system. These older systems work like "V0" lower engine pieces trying to support all the loads of a "V10,000" cylinder on nitrous (NOS) – a.k.a. "Hell's Motor."

LAW v. LAW

That is why legal professionals and the general public alike are interested in this new network and frequently question the Clean Law team of writers like: *"What is it, what is it for and how does it help us to have this SPN in our lives? "*

cleanlaw.today

Well, first of all, people generally tend to think of SPN as representing a kind of refined motor oil and network for cars that have extremely high mileage at the bottom of their engines and as an external coolant that is placed directly into the bearings of the engines, connecting rods, that is, the oil network becomes a "main vein". But the reality is very different. The SPN system is innovative and intellectual safety responsible for avoiding any type of damage that may cause any inconvenience to the safety of the engine. As mentioned above, this system is designed to significantly reduce the heat and friction generated by the pressures of law enforcement battles, which could lead to serious injury or even death, as well as psychological like confusion, depression, anxiety, and suicide attempts.

LAW LAW V.I.P. Best

So, why keep modifying a problem-ridden 180-degree “V” motor, when we can now pivot and take our cases to the more reliable and safer 360-degree “oil” solution? Introducing “heroes at law” practicing in the SPN and organically saving families. This is literally making a change, a better choice between "life or death" and "life with open access and choices." I think we all know the answer to this choice, but just the same, ***you decide!***

With Heaven’s oil, like guardian angels, there can be safety even within Hell’s motor and all its unbridled modifications. But you decide if protecting your roots with a side of empathy is vital or not to sustaining childhood, families, the future and community.

cleanlaw.today

The courthouse industry, that is, the legal industry represents approximately 2% of the gross domestic product (GDP) of the United States of America. And even though the legal industry accounted for $ 420 billion of U.S. GDP in 2019, the gap between "family law" and the "national legal system" was drastically diminishing and what seems like a tailspin. Because this specific circulation was supplemented by $ 11 billion from the federal government (Gormely). This results in a breakdown knowing that the engine rods are knocking. It's a lot of NOS used at the worst times.

The new "Child Safety File" oil is unique and different that federal NAS because they're customized for each molecule. You will see that not everyone has the time, patience, or resources to pay for this big change. But those that, if they can accept it, are the most significant areas of the United States to reside. It is, for example, like deciding to ride in a new Hummer or continue riding in a 200-year-old buggy. Another reason why it's vital to promote the development and use of the above-ground SPN system.

Organic Licensing, Counseling & Data

To prevent further breakdown of vital parts, Clean Law is an SPN together with family law offering B2B (business-to-business) licensing and B2C (business-to-customer) counseling. Both within it's very own SPN. That's its boundary outside of conventional law v. law systems. But the best part is the Clean Law business model. Not only is it like 23andMe which prevents physical health issues, the SPN prevents crime and donates 100% of the licensing proceeds to help other organic families survive and keep things together while they're experiencing V8 motors on NAS. It's not inside the conventional court and clerk's area, but outside and private. After all, we don't don't have to see the fighting and modified powers when we can feel it. That's what we're fixing. We only need to test, groom and shield out legal, social and psychological DNA knots where family roots used to be in order to keep us all running safely. That's the new economy. That's Heaven's oil.

cleanlaw.today

References

A Work in Process: Improving a Play Dough Process. (n.d.). Retrieved March 4, 2020, from https://www.eie.org/eie-curriculum/curriculum-units/work-process-improving-play-dough-process

Abel , L. K., & Rettig, M. (2006). State Statutes Providing for a Right to Counsel in Civil Cases. *Clearinghouse REVIEW Journal of Poverty Law and Policy*. Retrieved from https://www.brennancenter.org/sites/default/files/legacy/d/download_file_39169.pdf

Angelo, M. S. (2019). *High Conflict Separation/Divorce, Intimate Partner Violence and its Effects on Child Adjustment* (Doctoral dissertation, William James College).

Appadvice. (2019, April 26). Custody Transfer Log by College of Arts and Sciences - Southern Illinois University Edwardsville. Retrieved April 7, 2020, from https://appadvice.com/app/custody-transfer-log/1437923533

Austin, W. G., Fieldstone, L., & Pruett, M. K. (2013). Bench book for assessing parental gatekeeping in parenting disputes: Understanding the dynamics of gate closing and opening for the best interests of children. *Journal of Child Custody*, *10*(1), 1-16.

Austin, W. G., Pruett, M. K., Kirkpatrick, H. D., Flens, J. R., & Gould, J. W. (2013). Parental gatekeeping and child custody/child access evaluation: Part I: Conceptual framework, research, and application. *Family Court Review*, *51*(3), 485-501.

Basadur, M., Pringle, P., Speranzini, G., & Bacot, M. (2000). Collaborative problem solving through creativity in problem definition: Expanding the pie. *Creativity and Innovation Management*, *9*(1), 54-76.

Behm, M. (2005). Linking construction fatalities to the design for construction safety concept. *Safety science, 43*(8), 589-611.

Berland, L., Steingut, R., & Ko, P. (2014). High school student perceptions of the utility of the engineering design process: Creating opportunities to engage in engineering practices and apply math and science content. *Journal of Science Education and Technology, 23*(6), 705-720.

Buede, D. (2002, August). 6.2. 1 The Concepts of Systems Engineering as Practiced by the Wright Brothers. In *INCOSE International Symposium* (Vol. 12, No. 1, pp. 297-302).

Bollapragada, V., Khalid, M., & Wainner, S. (2005). *IPSec Vpn design.* Indianapolis, Ind: Cisco.

Greig, B. (2012, November 21). Few talk about the terrible toll marital breakdown can take on men's health. But here, one father reveals: 'The stress of divorce almost killed me'. Retrieved April 2, 2020, from https://www.dailymail.co.uk/femail/article-2236560/Few-talk-terrible-toll-marital-breakdown-mens-health-But-father-reveals-The-stress-divorce-killed-me.html

Cross, N. (2008). Engineering design methods: strategies for product design.

Compton, P., Yang, W., Lee, M., & Jansen, B. (1991). *Cornerstone cases in a dictionary approach to rule maintenance.* CSIRO, Division of Information Technology.

Davidson, J. L., & Jensen, C. (2013, June). Participatory design with older adults: an analysis of creativity in the design of mobile healthcare applications. In *Proceedings of the 9th ACM Conference on Creativity & Cognition* (pp. 114-123).

Family Law 2.0 [Interview by J. Gormely]. (August 3, 2020). Retrieved August 18, 2020, from https://www.savingfatherhood.org/36-family-law-2-0-with-aaron-wemple/.

Feinberg, M. E. (2003). The Internal Structure and Ecological Context of Coparenting: A Framework for Research and Intervention. *Parenting*, *3*(2), 95–131. doi: 10.1207/s15327922par0302_01

Hetherington, E. M., & Kelly, J. (2003). *For better or for worse: divorce reconsidered*. New York: W.W. Norton.

Hiniker, A., Sobel, K., & Lee, B. (2005). Co-Designing with Preschoolers Using Fictional Inquiry and Comicboarding.

Howard, T. J., Culley, S. J., & Dekoninck, E. (2008). Describing the creative design process by the integration of engineering design and cognitive psychology literature. *Design studies*, *29*(2), 160-180.

Jaha, A. A., Shatwan, F. B., & Ashibani, M. (n.d.). Proper Virtual Private Network (VPN) Solution.

Johnston, J. R. (1994). High-conflict divorce. *The future of children*, 165-182.

Kalter, N., Kloner, A., Schreier, S., & Okla, K. (1989). Predictors of children's postdivorce adjustment. *American Journal of Orthopsychiatry*, *59*(4), 605-618.

Katehi, L., National Academy of Engineering, National Research Council, & Committee on K-12 Engineering Education. (2009, September 8).

Engineering in K-12 Education: Understanding the Status and Improving the Prospects. Retrieved March 17, 2020, from https://www.nap.edu/catalog/12635/engineering-in-k-12-education-understanding-the-status-and-improving

Lamela, D., Figueiredo, B., Bastos, A., & Feinberg, M. (2015). Typologies of Post-divorce.

Lansford, L. (Director). (2019, October 17). *Tech Talk* [Video file]. Retrieved July 15, 2020, from https://www.amazon.com/Tech-Talk/dp/B07YNBH8K4

Coparenting and Parental Well-Being, Parenting Quality and Children's Psychological Adjustment. *Child Psychiatry & Human Development*, *47*(5), 716–728. doi: 10.1007/s10578-015-0604-5

Lebow, J., & Slesinger, N. (2016). Family therapy with families in intractable conflicts about child custody and visitation. In *Handbook of child custody* (pp. 291-301). Springer, Cham.

McFarlane, A. C. (2009). Military deployment: the impact on children and family adjustment and the need for care. *Current Opinion in Psychiatry*, *22*(4), 369-373.

Murdock, M. C., & Puccio, G. J. (1993). A contextual organizer for conducting creativity research. *Understanding and recognizing creativity: The emergence of a discipline*, 249-280.

National Research Council. (2012). *A framework for K-12 science education: Practices, crosscutting concepts, and core ideas*. National Academies Press.

Neighbors, B., Forehand, R., & Armistead, L. (1992). Is parental divorce a critical stressor for young adolescents? Grade point average as a case in point. *Adolescence*, *27*(107), 639–646.

Plan, E. T., & Khandani, S. (2005). Engineering design process.

Pruett, M. K., & Barker, R. (2009). Children of divorce: New trends and ongoing dilemmas.

Rogers, S. (2010, January 28). Divorce rates data, 1858 to now: how has it changed? Retrieved March 12, 2020, from https://www.theguardian.com/news/datablog/2010/jan/28/divorce-rates-marriage-ons

Section 8-Child Support Enforcement Program. (n.d.). Retrieved July 1,
    2020, from https://www.govinfo.gov/content/pkg/GPO-CPRT-
    108WPRT108-6/pdf/GPO-CPRT-108WPRT108-6-2-8.pdf

Schick, A. (2002). Behavioral and emotional differences between children
    of divorce and children from intact families: Clinical significance
    and mediating processes. *Swiss Journal of
    Psychology/Schweizerische Zeitschrift für Psychologie/Revue
    Suisse de Psychologie, 61*(1), 5.

Stinson, J. N., Jibb, L. A., Nguyen, C., Nathan, P. C., Maloney, A. M.,
    Dupuis, L. L., … Orr, M. (2013). Development and Testing of a
    Multidimensional iPhone Pain Assessment Application for
    Adolescents with Cancer. *Journal of Medical Internet
    Research, 15*(3).

Tashiro, T., Frazier, P., & Berman, M. (2006). Stress-related growth
    following divorce and relationship dissolution. *Handbook of
    divorce and relationship dissolution,* 361-384.

Terrell, S. R. (2015). *Writing a proposal for your dissertation: Guidelines
    and examples.* Guilford Publications.

Ullman, D. G. (2010). *The mechanical design process: Part 1.* McGraw-
    Hill.

Wallerstein, J. S., Lewis, J., & Blakeslee, S. (2014). *The unexpected
    legacy of divorce: a 25 year landmark study.* New York: Hachette
    Books.

Wemple, A. W. (2018, August 22). The CLU Story: United Parents Guide.
    Retrieved March 28, 2020, from
    https://issuu.com/cleanlaw/docs/the-clu-story-book.pptx

Wemple, A. W. (2018). *Family Law 2.0.* St. Louis, MO: Clean Law.

Wemple, A. W. (2019). *2020 Family Bill.* St. Louis, MO: Clean Law.

Wemple, A. W. (2020, February 3). Retrieved from
    https://www.cleanlaw.today/post/forward

Yoon, C., Cole, C. A., & Lee, M. P. (2009). Consumer decision making
    and aging: Current knowledge and future directions. *Journal of
    Consumer Psychology, 19*(1), 2-16.

Zorza, R., Morhar, L., Greacen, J., Lash, K., Alteneder, K., & Danser, R.
    (2017). Resource: Title IV-D Funding Resource Guide (SRLN 2014)
    Retrieved May 24, 2020, from https://www.srln.org/node/53/
    resource-title-iv-d-funding-resource-guide-srln-2014

"A new bottomless cup of good –

childhood safety,

Family sustainability

And community re-developments!"

www.ingramcontent.com/pod-product-compliance
Lightning Source LLC
Chambersburg PA
CBHW05052828280326
41933CB00011B/1509